WHY THE JEWS?

WHY THE JEWS?

THE NEED TO SCAPEGOAT

MAREK HALTER

TRANSLATED BY GRACE McQUILLAN

ARCADE PUBLISHING • NEW YORK

First English-language Edition

Originally published in France under the title *Pourquoi les Juifs?* by Michel Lafon Publishing.

Arcade Publishing books may be purchased in bulk at special discounts for sales promotion, corporate gifts, fund-raising, or educational purposes. Special editions can also be created to specifications. For details, contact the Special Sales Department, Arcade Publishing, 307 West 36th Street, 11th Floor, New York, NY 10018 or arcade@skyhorsepublishing.com.

Arcade Publishing® is a registered trademark of Skyhorse Publishing, Inc.®, a Delaware corporation.

Visit our website at www.arcadepub.com.

10 9 8 7 6 5 4 3 2 1

Library of Congress Cataloging-in-Publication Data

Names: Halter, Marek, author. | McQuillan, Grace, translator.
Title: Why the Jews? : the need to scapegoat / Marek Halter, Grace McQuillan.
Other titles: Pourquoi les Juifs? English
Description: New York, NY : Skyhorse Publishing, [2021]
Identifiers: LCCN 2020048099 (print) | LCCN 2020048100 (ebook) | ISBN 9781951627430 (hardcover) | ISBN 9781951627584 (epub)
Subjects: LCSH: Jews–Persecutions–Europe, Western–History. | Antisemitism–Europe, Western–History. | Anti-Jewish propaganda–Europe, Western–History.
Classification: LCC DS146.E85 H3513 2021 (print) | LCC DS146.E85 (ebook) | DDC 305.892/404–dc23
LC record available at https://lccn.loc.gov/2020048099
LC ebook record available at https://lccn.loc.gov/2020048100

Jacket design by Brian Peterson

Printed in the United States of America

In memory of Clara Halter, my forever companion.

The topic of this book was a source of disagreement,
but perhaps, presented this way,
we might have seen eye to eye. Who knows?

CONTENTS

CONTENTS

1

THE RETURN OF ANTI-SEMITISM?

Hatred for Jews is showing its face again, everywhere, to staggering degrees.

We thought an awareness of the Holocaust would be our greatest stronghold against fanaticism. We were wrong. With the disappearance of witnesses and the erosion of time, tempers are raging, stoked by a joint assault by the propaganda of a few totalitarian states looking for enemies and a tireless mob of negationists, racists, xenophobes, and conspiracy theorists of all kinds on social media—who are helped, it must be said, by the ignorance of the majority of our contemporaries and the passivity of a few who know what is happening but are too afraid to come forward.

Seventy-five years after the Second World War and its tens of millions of deaths, seventy-five years after hatred of Jews decimated a people several thousand years old—a people I belong to—seventy-five years after swearing "This will never happen again!" in an almost unanimous voice, "this" is spilling from our gutters.

The situation today is most concerning in Western European countries, the part of Europe that fashioned the very notion of the rights of man. In Germany, for example, where until recently the word "anti-Semite" was still unpronounceable because of Nazism, violent acts against Jews increased by 70 percent in 2018 alone.

According to the European Jewish Congress (CJE) in Paris, three out of four Poles believe "Jews talk too much about the Holocaust," 25 percent of Hungarians think "Jews want to weaken the national culture by supporting immigration," and 72 percent of Ukrainians claim that "Jews are too great a burden on the economy." In England, the homeland of Benjamin Disraeli, anti-Semitism manifests itself in everyday life: in poorer neighborhoods first and foremost, but also in universities and within the Labour Party. Even the United States, home to the largest Jewish community in the world and a country that over the years, thanks to powerful organizations like B'nai B'rith, the Anti-Defamation

League, the American Jewish Committee, and the World Jewish Congress and its unique network of education and mutual assistance, has been able to fill the role that the Babylonian community played in the Diaspora at the end of the sixth century BCE.

Yet in this same country, where two centuries ago Portuguese-American Jewish writer Mordecai Manuel Noah had wanted to establish a Jewish state, when American Jewish college students were asked, "Have you witnessed or personally experienced anti-Semitism?" 54 percent said yes, according to a poll conducted for the American Jewish Committee.

In 1825, Mordecai Manuel Noah purchased land on Grand Island in New York. In front of an enthusiastic crowd, he laid the first stone for a city he called Ararat, from the name of the mountain between Turkey and Armenia on which, the Bible tells us, God made Noah's ark run aground at the end of the Flood.

In the United States, where just yesterday my American friends said, "That will never happen *here*," two deadly attacks on synagogues in Pittsburgh, Pennsylvania, and Poway, California, in 2018 and 2019 stunned American Jews who until now had felt safe. This was followed in December 2019 by a shooting at a kosher grocery store in

Jersey City, New Jersey, and a stabbing at the home of a rabbi in Monsey, New York, during a Hanukkah celebration. This attack led President Donald Trump to sign an executive order on December 11, 2019, aimed at fighting anti-Semitism on American campuses, the first in the country's history.

But the danger is most immediate in Europe. In writing these lines, I've stumbled upon an interview Primo Levi gave in 1983 to Anna Bravo and Federico Cereja (*Le Devoir de mémoire* [The Duty of Memory] [Paris: Mille et une nuits, 2000]). Levi seems wary of what appears to be a lack of clarity in the Jewish community about the wave of anti-Judaism at the time. He was right.

How do we alert our friends and neighbors? How do we make them understand that even with multiple media sources and noble initiatives, we are still not immune to evil?

"I have often been to talk in schools," Levi says, "and I've found interest, horror, pity, sometimes incredulity, amazement, incomprehension . . . I wouldn't know what general diagnosis to propose, at present I feel that too much time has passed, I don't willingly accept invitations to schools anymore because I feel like an old survivor, like one of Garibaldi's men, a 'greybeard' essentially."[1]

---

1   English translation: Marco Belpoliti and Robert Gordon, eds., *The Voice of Memory* (New York: The New Press, 2001).

I know what he means. I wonder what dear Primo would say if he knew that in France—the country where non-Jews, it should be remembered, saved two-thirds of the Jewish community during the Occupation—seventy-five years after the liberation of Auschwitz, according to figures from the French Ministry of the Interior and the SPCJ (Service de Protection de la Communauté Juive, the Jewish Community Security Service), 541 acts against Jews were recorded in 2018, an increase of 74 percent from 2017. These acts represented half of the hate crimes documented on French soil.

A report from the Kantor Center for the Study of Contemporary European Jewry states that in 2018, the number of Jews murdered worldwide in a single year was the highest it has been in several decades.

The year 2019 is no better. Take the month of February, for example: on the tenth, the front window of a Bagelstein restaurant in Île Saint-Louis in Paris is spray-painted with an enormous *Juden* ("Jews" in German), just like under the Nazi regime. On the eleventh, swastikas are drawn over portraits of Simone Veil painted on the walls of Paris by street artist Christian Guémy (a.k.a. C215). On the thirteenth, a plaque at the entrance to a school in Maisons-Alfort (Val-de-Marne), in memory of Jewish children deported during the Nazi occupation, is shattered. On the nineteenth, some eighty graves in a Jewish cemetery in Quatzenheim in Alsace (Bas-Rhin) are defaced with swastikas. The same day, the outer wall of the Bry-sur-Marne synagogue (Val-de-Marne) is tagged with the inscription *Mort au Juif*—"Death to the Jew." On the twentieth, anti-Semitic graffiti is discovered in a memory garden in the Champagne-au-Mont-d'Or cemetery near Lyon . . .

The Jewish community in France is alarmed and decides to take action. It organizes a gathering with anti-racist groups on the Place de la République in Paris. This only draws fifteen thousand people, the majority of whom are Jewish. I launch an appeal to Muslims with the Imam of Drancy, Hassen Chalghoumi. The result: barely 250 of us march behind a banner with the slogan "Muslims against Anti-Semitism" written in French and Arabic.

*

In 1979, Simone Veil and I were at a dinner concluding a colloquium on the Holocaust that we had been invited to by Willy Brandt, then Federal Chancellor and leader of the German Social Democratic Party. Brandt remarked that in his opinion, the fascists had come to power in Germany not because of their number, but because at the time there hadn't been enough supporters of the democratic system over the totalitarian system.

Supporters of the democratic system today appear to have better things to do than protest against anti-Semitism, though this term may not be the most appropriate to describe certain people's ambition to eradicate Jews from their neighborhoods, their countries, and from the very planet that millions of young people are willing to defend from climate risks.

The word "anti-Semitism," used in the sense of "hostility toward Jews," was first used in 1879 by German polemist Wilhelm Marr, who extrapolated the research findings of linguist and Indian studies specialist Friedrich Max Müller (1823–1900). According to Müller, who was one of the first academics to compare Semitic and Aryan religions—the veneration of God in history versus the veneration of God in nature—the word "Semite" referred to speakers of "Semitic" languages like Akkadian, Phoenician, Hebrew, Arabic, and Amharic, as opposed to the so-called "Aryan" languages.

The word "Semite" itself comes from Shem, one of Noah's three sons, who, like his father, was saved from the Flood by the ark in which they took refuge.

Today, Arabs are the largest Semitic group, so for them to call themselves "anti-Semitic" would be a flagrant demonstration of self-hatred. For most of us, though, the anti-Semite is—above all—a person who dislikes Jews.

2

WHY SUCH HATRED?

Where does this hatred come from? When did it appear? And for what reasons?

"Difference engenders hatred," Stendhal said simply. All differences, really? The Sikh, for example, with his long beard and turban wound around the top of his head: Does he arouse hatred or curiosity? Yet when the chief prosecutor at the Eichmann trial in Jerusalem, Gideon Hausner, tried to understand how this hatred for Jews could lead to such a massacre, historian Salo Baron responded: "People dislike the unlike."

We know it is not good to hate the other solely because he is what he is. There are even laws today condemning those who do not respect difference. But can hatred be prohibited by a simple vote in Parliament? Marie de Flavigny, Countess d'Agoult (1805-1876), one of whose daughters would marry composer Richard Wagner, said, "The worst kinds of hatreds are those that are so vile and base that one must lower oneself to fight them."[2] Fighting hatred with intelligence, knowledge, and the constant reminder of morality is not enough. And if we stoop to the level of the gutter, we would lose credibility. So how can we get out of this dilemma?

Accusations of all kinds against Jews litter the shelves of libraries, fueling the knee-jerk reactions and fantasies of our contemporaries. "For the Jews," Guillaume Erner writes, "everything begins in history and ends in metaphysics."[3] The reason for this hatred toward one of the world's most ancient peoples—a people that has been able to preserve its identity in spite of forced displacements and massacres, a "fossilized" people according to Toynbee, an "indefinable" people in the words of my friend Vladimir Jankélévitch—has yet to be explained. So if indeed the Jews are inclined to the metaphysical, it is precisely because of this permanent hostility, the causes of which can only be understood through

---

2   English translation by Grace McQuillan.

3   Guillaume Erner, *Expliquer l'antisémitisme* (Paris: PUF, 2015). Translation by Grace McQuillan.

transcendence. In this case, anti-Semitism would pertain to what Kant calls the sublime: "[That which] is absolutely great [...], beyond all comparison great."[4]

The very term "anti-Semitism," a phrase that has accompanied me since childhood, marks a victory of imagination over understanding. And yet, for as long as I can remember, I have known it is a label for people who don't like me. Whether or not I'm kind to them. Anti-Semites reject me simply because I am a Jew.

In Warsaw, where I was born, this didn't pose a problem for me. I was a Jew and lived among Jews. I didn't see the people who weren't Jews and who didn't like me. I only knew they existed. At the time, in a city of a million people, 370,000 were Jewish, with their restaurants and newspapers, their cinemas and theaters, their poor and their rich, their thieves and their beggars, their political parties and their language—Yiddish, my language, my nostalgia. It was not the ghetto. Not yet. But the hostile environment required Jews to keep to themselves. Hatred separated them from the rest of the population more effectively than all the walls.

Romain Gary describes completing part of his studies in Warsaw in the 1920s. "Even at the time, there were already

---

4   English translation: Paul Crowther, *The Kantian Sublime: From Morality to Art* (Oxford: Oxford University Press, 1989).

special benches for Jews to sit on. I went to sit on one of those benches and got beaten up for it."[5]

What is true for individuals is also true for whole peoples. Because they are being persecuted, they eventually ask themselves why. And they begin to doubt themselves. "It is probably not without reason that this poor Israel has passed its life as a people in being massacred. Since all nations and all ages have persecuted them, there must have been some motive," Ernest Renan kindly writes in chapter 11 of his *Antichrist*.[6] In the face of such readings, Jews were left with the choice between suicide or some kind of compensation, taking a certain pride in this suffering: "People don't like us because we're better, more hardworking, more honest. Even if the others, the anti-Semites, won't admit it, *we* know it and are comforted."

In Poland, when a prince and his retinue rode through a Jewish village and beat an old man, he did not protest. He just nodded like someone who pitied the man who had to beat a person like him to assert his own power. For the 3.5 million Jews who were living in the country at the

---

5   English translation: Romain Gary, *Le judaïsme n'est pas une question de sang* (Paris: L'Herne, 2007), interview published in *Le Figaro*, July 4, 1967. Translation by Grace McQuillan.

6   English translation: Ernest Renan, *The History of the Origins of Christianity Book IV–The Antichrist* (Sacramento, CA: Franklin Classics, an imprint of Creative Media Partners, 2018).

time, knowledge and learning were the only things of value. Understanding a parable from the Talmud or being able to interpret a passage from the Torah was worth a thousand times more than finding one's name on an electoral list.

And so, over the centuries, a particular spirit developed: the Jewish spirit, with its rich literature, folklore, music, and singular humor. For Jews, humor is a form of resistance. According to Henri Bergson, "Several have defined man as 'an animal which laughs.' They might equally well have defined him as an animal which is laughed at [...]."[7] Bergson adds that unless we stifle our emotions (laughter's "greatest enemy"), it is difficult to laugh at a person who inspires pity in us.

And so, as much to escape from pity as from hatred, to forestall and disarm the irony, sarcasm, and caricatures that are heaped upon them, Jews invented another category of laughter: self-deprecation, or laughing at oneself. This laughter, which is called "Jewish humor" by Sigmund Freud in his book *Jokes and Their Relation to the Unconscious*, plays on the transfer of words and situations. Example: When the first roundups of Jews in France were announced, playwright Tristan Bernard declared: "I myself belong to this people that has often been called 'the elected' . . . That is,

---

7 English translation: John Mullarkey and Keith Ansell Pearson, eds., *Key Writings–Henri Bergson* (London: Bloomsbury Publishing, 2014).

'waiting for the second ballot.'"[8] And upon arriving with his wife at the Drancy transit camp, the antechamber of Auschwitz: "Until now we have lived in fear, from now on we will live in hope."

*

My family escaped the Nazi ghetto and death thanks to two Catholic friends of my father—two activists, like him, from the printers' union. One night they came. Their repeated knocks on the door woke me up.

They offered to accompany us to the Soviet border. The following night, we encountered a German patrol.

"*Jude?* Jewish?"

I remember the question, not the person who asked it. The beam of the flashlight he was pointing at me blinded me.

My mother had told me hundreds of times: "If German soldiers stop us and ask you if you're Jewish, you say no." In my childhood subconscious, the acknowledgment of my Jewishness was obvious, essential. I couldn't think of any danger greater than being nothing at all.

---

8   English translation: Herbert Lottman, *The Left Bank: Writers, Artists, and Politics from the Popular Front to the Cold War* (Chicago: University of Chicago Press, 1998).

Neglecting the deadly threat that the soldier's question carried, I responded: "Jewish? Yes, of course!"

Our Catholic friends burst out laughing. The Nazis did the same.

"Let them pass," said the highest-ranking soldier, "the child is joking! A Jew would never turn himself in."

My mother concluded from this that the best lie was the truth.

*

The Soviets sent us to Moscow, which would also soon be under bombs. Stalin deported us, along with one million others, to Almaty in Kazakhstan. Then to Kokand in Uzbekistan, also in Central Asia. Even there, so far from everything else, people didn't like Jews very much. One day I was accosted by a band of troublemakers.

"So, little Jew," one of them yelled, "are you happy to be here?"

"Little Jew?" I answered. "Am I so different from all of you?"

With that, I pulled down my pants.

"Look!" I said. "I have the same weenie as you!"

Surprised and horrified by this unexpected gesture in the middle of the street, assaulted by my little penis, circumcised just like theirs—they were Muslim—they took off running. As if I had pulled a machine gun out of my trousers.

*

Even in France, where we settled in 1950, people were bothered by my assertion of my Judaism, something that was so natural for me. The French back then wanted to forget the ruptures and shame of the war. People preferred the word "Israelite" over the word "Jew." The memory of deportation was fresh, and the stain of the yellow star was very much present. Even among the most progressive and open left-wing intellectuals, Judaism proved a difficult subject. It was in this context that Jean-Paul Sartre's *Anti-Semite and Jew* appeared.[9] I was strongly urged to read it.

To be honest, this essay left me profoundly uneasy. I was flattered that such a renowned and respected philosopher had made the effort to think about the Jews' situation and, in a way, about my own. But his conclusions appalled me. In essence, Sartre argues that the Jew and Jewish identity are defined through the gaze of the other. Which would mean that I am only Jewish thanks to the existence of the anti-Semite!

---

9   Jean-Paul Sartre, *Anti-Semite and Jew*, trans. George J. Becker (New York: Schocken Books, 1948).

At seventeen, self-assurance is king. From my friends, I managed to procure Sartre's address in Saint-Germain-des-Prés. One autumn afternoon, completely unannounced, I knocked on his door.

A short and affable man with an unsettling gaze, Jean-Paul Sartre was unoffended by this untimely visit. He showed me in and we sat down, if my memory is correct, in a room that to me seemed small and completely saturated with furniture and books. At that time, people were still impressed by "survivors" of the Warsaw ghetto. For someone like Sartre, this part of my history opened doors and abolished barriers. He listened to me patiently while I tried to express my critique as clearly as possible. To me, my reasoning seemed irrefutable.

How could the author of *Being and Nothingness*, who claimed that man is condemned, without recourse, to absolute freedom—how could he take that very freedom away from me, a Jew? How could he think that my identity depended entirely on my own executioner's perception of me?

"On the contrary," he countered in his thin voice, "in this book I only speak about inauthentic Jews. The ones who let other people influence their attitudes."

"So? Who are authentic Jews? What defines them?"

"Well, I suppose those are the religious Jews, no? Those Jews have *chosen* their place and their image. They are fully capable of exercising their freedom. The Jewish identity others try to impose on them has no hold over them."

"But, since you appear to equate Jews with religion, what about non-religious Jews? There are millions of them. They too have the right to an identity and the exercise of their free will."

For Sartre, as for so many others before him, the word "Jew" designated a (persecuted) religious group and not a people. This is contrary to Kant, for whom "Strictly speaking, Judaism is not a religion at all but simply the union of a number of individuals who [...] established themselves into a community under purely political laws."[10]

There was a brief silence. His overly pale face lit up with a smile.

"Yes . . . My reflections are those of a *goy*, someone who looks at Jews from the outside."

He thrust his hand in my direction, a little sharply, as he often did, and added, "So it is up to someone on the inside to paint the portrait of an authentic Jew, one who chooses his identity for himself and freely takes a stand as one."

---

10 English translation: Kim Treiger-Bar-Am, *Positive Freedom and the Law* (New York: Routledge, 2019).

Was he insinuating that a young man like me could take up this yoke?

Even though I felt like I left that interview still carrying my entire problem, just as heavy and knotted as it had been an hour before, that was the moment I began turning over in my mind the questions I am asking in this book.

What does it mean to be Jewish? What is Jewishness? What is Judaism?

3

THE JEWISH ENIGMA

In spite of the thousands of books written about them, Jews and Judaism remain, for most of our contemporaries—and even for a number of Jews themselves—a mystery. To begin with, do people know how to describe the difference between an Israelite, a Jew, and an Israeli? I doubt it! An Israeli is someone with an Israeli passport. That goes without saying. But the Israelite? Is this someone who practices the Jewish religion? But then, what is a Jew? And what about a Jew who doesn't practice religion? Yet we are all referred to indiscriminately as "Jews." And everyone seems to have some idea of what this means.

What exactly is the identity of the Jew, this person, our neighbor, our fellow man, who constantly puzzles his peers by claiming to have a history that is at once entirely unique and yet intertwined to such an extent with the history of the world that it has become one of its pillars? What is the identity of this people, confronted from its very beginnings by the One God, Creator of the world, when he appeared to Abraham over four thousand years ago in the distant land of Ur of the Chaldeans? This people, whose extraordinary longevity bewilders and intrigues because most of the ancient nations it rubbed shoulders with (the Assyrians, the Arameans, the Midianites, and the Carthaginians) have, as Chateaubriand remarks, disappeared long ago from our memories, regardless of their past power and glory.[11]

Who is this mythical Jew who "draws the eye," really? This Jew, who is either loved or hated without people giving much thought to actually knowing him? This Jew, whom some people—not many, it must be said—endow with a thousand positive qualities while others, unfortunately the majority, pile every flaw upon him? Flaws among which his love of money ranks the highest, for weren't Jews the

---

11 English translation: François-René de Chateaubriand, *Travels to Jerusalem and the Holy Land: Through Egypt, Volume 2*, trans. Frederic Shoberl (London: J. L. Cox and Sons, 1835).

first moneylenders? The very same ones who became the Rothschilds of today? Ah, the force of ignorance!

To Catholics of the Middle Ages, money was unclean: consider the story of the thirty pieces of silver Judas supposedly received in exchange for denouncing Christ. So kings, princes, and nobility used the Jews to manage their wealth. This allowed these few privileged Jews to finance community assistance organizations to help the most destitute among them and thus maintain the solidarity demanded by the Talmud.

Faced with the thriving development of lending establishments run by Jews and Lombards, in 1462 the Catholics invented a charitable lending institution known as the *mont de piété* ("mount of piety"), which was officially recognized by Pope Leo X in 1515. Therefore, contrary to what people may believe, it was the *Catholics* who agreed to set aside their qualms and open the first banks: the Medici family first, followed later by Protestants in Bordeaux and Amsterdam.

Today, if the anti-Semitic writings on the internet are to be believed, most of the world's banks are controlled by Jewish families.

Yasser Arafat, whom I knew personally, was also convinced that Jews held financial power. He even believed that John Davison Rockefeller was Jewish. I had to purchase a *Who's Who* in order to prove to him that the Rockefeller family was Protestant, and I suspect that he still didn't believe me. When people want to kill a dog, they first accuse it of having rabies.

These were the kinds of accusations Robespierre attempted to address in a 1789 speech before the National Constituent Assembly on the Jews' right to vote: "The Jews' vices are born of the degradation you have plunged them into. They will be good when they can find some advantage in so being!"[12]

*

Two hundred and thirty years later, as I was leaving a lecture hall in Bordeaux where I was presenting my memoirs, *Je rêvais de changer le monde*, a young woman asked me, "Why the Jews?"

She easily could have asked, "Why the Arabs?" "Why the blacks?" "Why the homosexuals?" "Why the Romani?"

Realizing the vagueness of her question, she added, "Why is it *always* the Jews?"

I was perturbed. "Is the image of the Jew so deeply rooted in our subconscious that it devours the Jew himself, just as Freud says?"

---

12 English translation: Léon Poliakov, *The History of Anti-Semitism, Volume 3: From Voltaire to Wagner*, trans. Miriam Kochan (Philadelphia: University of Pennsylvania Press, 2003).

For the anti-Semite, the word "Jew" means simply "stranger," or "other." And yet if we return to Freud's concept of *Unheimlich*, this other is "something which is secretly familiar"![13] Like the surface of a lily pad, it hides a deep root that, in this case, plunges into the depths of the collective unconscious of a society where a social imagination forged over centuries has settled.

I am therefore persuaded that in order to understand humanity, one must begin not with the general, but with the particular. Universalism, contrary to what Voltaire believed, produces no added tolerance. It brings with it its own dogma, devises a single culture, and inflicts it on the world in every language. People cannot be forced to be happy against their will.

I acknowledge that, after the revocation of the Edict of Nantes in 1685, it was brave of Voltaire to publish a *Treatise on Tolerance*.[14] But today the word "tolerance" bothers me. I like "recognize" better than "tolerate": I recognize the other as different from me and I ask him to respect me, I who am different from him, just as he would wish me to respect him.

At present, the French do not understand why, when they have granted the Muslims who live among them the

---

13 English translation: Sigmund Freud, *The Uncanny*, trans. David McLintock (London: Penguin, 2003).

14 Originally published by Frères Cramer, 1763.

same rights that they demand for themselves, this group still clings to its difference. This is perhaps one of the reasons for the mounting Islamophobia in our country and may also explain the misunderstanding between the words "integration" and "assimilation." Muslims in France are, for the vast majority, integrated. The incredible number of comedians of North African descent that make us laugh in French is proof of this. But they are not assimilated. Why would they be? Their history and ours have been closely intertwined ever since they have lived in France, of course. But before that? Must they forget everything to become good French people? When I arrived in France, the debate on foreigners settling in the country was defined in terms of assimilation. That was how it was—the immigrant had to become like everyone else. Today, this idea is shocking.

In early 1984, I had a visit from a few young people, most of whom were children of immigrants. They wanted unity in difference and a multifaceted society that looked like them. They had taken part in the Beurs' March in 1983, when thirty children of immigrants marched out of Marseille and grew to a group of tens of thousands by the time they arrived in Paris two months later.

They had already formed an organization: SOS Racisme. They even had a slogan and a logo: an open yellow hand with the words *Touche pas à mon pote*, or "Don't touch my friend." A modern translation of "Love your neighbor as yourself." They already had everything to succeed and didn't really need me, except perhaps to get themselves noticed.

On that day in 1984, the greatest antiracist movement of postwar France was born.

SOS Racisme offered young people from the *banlieues*, the housing projects—dropouts, idle, sometimes on drugs— another experience. I was happy to be a part of it. When, a year later, over four hundred thousand young people filled the Place de la Concorde to celebrate the Fête des Potes de SOS Racisme—a sort of French Woodstock—I was unsurprised by the extent of their success.

Did the actions of these young people change our society? I don't know. What I am certain of is that, just like in May 1968, they at least made people think. And I confess that I was proud to count Jewish students among the founders of this enormous movement against racism. To me, however, racism and anti-Semitism are not on the same plane. Of course, both of them kill. But the motivations and objectives of the murderers are different.

*

Racism is the hatred of the other who is seen as dissimilar in appearance. The word "racism," amply theorized about by

Count Joseph Arthur de Gobineau, a Frenchman, appeared for the first time at the end of the nineteenth century in the writing of Gaston Méry, another Frenchman. Hatred of the other, though, which is based on difference of any kind, is far more ancient.

If, as historian Marc Bloch said, "every man seeks the reflection of his own image in the other," imagine the surprise of those early tribes who went seeking new pastureland or, later, that of the first explorers who discovered a humanity with appearances, customs, behaviors, hierarchies, and gods that were different from their own. Viewed by whites as creations of the devil, blacks feared the Europeans who wielded lightning and brought with them misfortune and diseases. And what about Europe's perpetual encounters with Asia? And with Native Americans? The Church was left wondering whether men with copper skin had a soul.

Anti-Semitism, on the other hand, expresses the hatred of an other who is similar in appearance. Jews are whites among whites, blacks among blacks, Indians among Indians—in Mumbai, Kochi, and Malabar where they are called *Bene Israel*—and Chinese among Chinese—traces of them can still be found in Kaifeng in the Henan province. Physically, they do not stand out from the majority of the population: in the eyes of anti-Semites, this makes them all the more worrying.

The existence of the Jewish people, therefore, poses several problems. If Judaism could be reduced to a religion, that would be one thing. But in fact, as Jean-Paul Sartre remarks, it is the secular Jews that bother people most. When a man describes himself as strictly German, Russian, or French, one need only appeal to his territorial patriotism and nationalist sensibilities to make him toe the line. Every additional dimension, cultural or religious, especially if it belongs to a minority, makes the individual more complex and more difficult to convince and manipulate. This is why the totalitarian system hates multifaceted people so much, why it is suspicious of intellectuals, immigrants, and anyone who is familiar with other horizons and cultures.

While Jews are multifaceted by definition—in France, for instance, they are French and Jewish first, then either religious or not—they never appear uprooted because they are rooted in the Book. It is through the Text of the Bible that they dialogue with one another and find their common history and values.

Anti-Semites place no trust in Jews, even those who have converted to other religions. Nor do they have confidence in pogroms and ghettos, the latter an invention of the Doge of Venice in 1516. Instead, it is by burning their Books that anti-Semites try on a regular basis to cut Jews off from their roots. When they can, they also burn bodies, individually or en masse. Basically, the anti-Semite, or rather the anti-Jew, is under no illusions: he does not try to reform the Jews because he knows, like Bernanos, that for each one of them it is "not a question of conquering, but of enduring as long as possible."[15]

*

I am paging through Léon Poliakov's impressive *History of Anti-Semitism*,[16] which in several volumes describes the evolution of this hatred that Jews cannot shake off, and I realize that I cannot find an answer to the "Why?" of my young audience member in Bordeaux.

And so, as often happens in the face of an injustice that we do not know how to prevent or repair, I feel like shouting. Just like Abbé Pierre, the famous defender of social outcasts, who one day in the winter of 1954, heartbroken at not being able to save the people dying of cold outside, shouted into the microphone of a radio presenter, "My friends, help me!"

---

15 Georges Bernanos, *La Grande Peur des bien-pensants* [The Great Fear of Right-Thinking People] (Paris: Grasset, 1931). Translation by Grace McQuillan.

16 Léon Poliakov, *The History of Anti-Semitism*, trans. Richard Howard et al. (Philadelphia: University of Pennsylvania Press, 2003).

Half a century after him, I too found myself shouting, literally, into a microphone. It was January 2006, just after the kidnapping and murder of Ilan Halimi, a young French Jew who was tortured to death by a group calling themselves the Gang of Barbarians. I went with my friends from SOS Racisme to the place his executioners had left him to die. That same evening, I was supposed to present my books on television. I arrived at the studio trembling with rage, sickened that in our republican and democratic France, someone could murder a young man for being Jewish.

Sitting across from the host, I said that I would like to share my anger with the French people watching so each of them would understand the dangers of anti-Semitism. He encouraged me to go ahead. In that moment I realized that the speech I had prepared would only be added to all the others people would hear. So I asked the viewers to shout with me. And I shouted. I thought I was alone, but there were millions of us.

But shouting is not a remedy. Not even a roadblock. All it can do is awaken the conscience sleeping in every one of us. But to do what?

As in medicine, fighting the problem requires first knowing the causes. Certain diseases only appear under specific conditions: when the body is weakened, for example, or in a state of stress. Hence sociologist Émile Durkheim's remark during the Dreyfus affair: "When society undergoes suffering, it feels the need to find someone whom it can hold responsible for its sickness."[17]

---

17 English translation: Steve Fenton, *Durkheim and Modern Sociology* (Cambridge: Cambridge University Press, 1984).

4

THE JEW, A PERFECT SCAPEGOAT

When everything is going well, when you have a good job, when your wife loves you and your children have good grades in school, even if your neighbor has strange customs and cooking that fills the stairwell with an odor you find troubling—as noted by Jacques Chirac in his speech in Orléans addressed to supporters of his party, Rally for the Republic (RPR)—you will still find yourself in a good mood. You may even take an interest in this neighbor's unique history, taste his food, and enrich your own culture. But as soon as your child gets sick or you lose your job, this same neighbor, because he is not one of you, will be suspected of being the direct or indirect cause of your misfortune. He thus becomes a "scapegoat."

This term, whose origins date back to ancient Greece (*pharmakos*: a person burned as a sacrifice to atone for another's wrongdoing), appears more specifically in the Bible in a ritual described in Leviticus. On the Day of Atonement, Yom Kippur, the temple priests would cast lots to select a goat that they would load with all the people's sins before sending it to die in the desert.

In *Sin and Fear: The Emergence of a Western Guilt Culture, 13th–18th Centuries*, Jean Delumeau describes how during the Black Death in the Middle Ages, which devastated entire regions, lepers were accused of poisoning the wells and were hunted down to be punished for their evil deeds.[18] The lepers had become scapegoats. But these punitive campaigns also extended, "naturally," to Jewish communities. Why?

Historian Hugh Trevor-Roper explains in *The Rise of Christian Europe* that the fourteenth century had in fact already seen another form of popular revolt: anti-Semitism. "Indebted peasants in the country, starving craftsmen in the towns, looked for scapegoats in their midst and found the Jews."[19]

But the question remains unanswered: "Why the Jews?"

---

18 Jean Delumeau, *Sin and Fear: The Emergence of a Western Guilt Culture, 13th–18th Centuries*, trans. Eric Nicholson (London: St. Martin's Press, 1991).

19 English translation: Hugh Trevor-Roper, *The Rise of Christian Europe* (London: Thames and Hudson, 1965).

*

"Because of their arrogance," their claim that they are "the elected people" of God, anti-Semites say. Bullshit! There is no question of election in any Text. "[T]he LORD set His heart on you and chose you [...] because the LORD favored you and kept the oath He made to your fathers," Deuteronomy 7:7–8 says.[20] And the prophet Amos adds (3:2): "That is why I will call you to account for all your iniquities." This is a reminder: the Jews are not better than other people. But, since they have been "chosen" by God to be the guardians of the Law, guardians of the Ten Commandments—a sacred mission, in other words—they have a duty, one that each Jew imposes on himself and without which he would cease to be Jewish.

This permanence, this attachment to the Law, which for certain rabbis precedes even God, arouses suspicion and discomfort. Having a neighbor who is constantly holding up a mirror to our faces, even if it's with the best intentions, and especially when it's with the best intentions, is irritating. Then comes the rejection, the violence. Finally, after

---

20 *Tanakh: The Holy Scriptures* (Philadelphia: The Jewish Publication Society, 1985). All subsequent citations are from this version.

having chased this neighbor away, sometimes after killing him, comes the guilty conscience.

How "the world loathes these indefatigable victims," Albert Camus writes ironically in his collection of articles entitled *Actuelles II*, "because they are the ones who spoil everything, and it is entirely their fault that humanity has an unpleasant odor."[21] Israeli psychiatrist Zvi Rex goes even further, saying that "the Germans will never forgive the Jews for Auschwitz."

*

It is a fact: the scapegoat is indispensable to society. Léon Bloy, in *Le Salut par les Juifs* ("Salvation Through the Jews"), defends this idea, but as anti-Semitic as he is, he nevertheless wishes to keep the Jews alive, as a permanent reminder of the death of Christ which, according to him, they are responsible for.[22] Except that hatred does not restrict itself to public utility. It seeks the annihilation of its object. "Death to the Jews!" the slogan we often hear during anti-Semitic protests today, therefore proves inescapable.

---

21 Albert Camus, *Actuelles II: Chroniques 1948–1953*. (Paris: Gallimard, 1953). Translation by Grace McQuillan.

22 Léon Bloy, *Le Salut par les Juifs* (Paris: Gallimard, 1953).

*

Sarcelles, July 20, 2014: a town of sixty thousand people. The inhabitants of this suburb, half an hour from Paris, are diverse and different from one another, but they live in perfect harmony: Tamils, Turks, Kurds, Pakistanis, Sri Lankans, Comorians, Romanians, Copts, Chaldeans, Christians of course, Jews, Muslims; each group has its own neighborhood. Everyone meets on the aptly named Place du Souvenir-Français and at the market on Avenue Frédéric-Joliot-Curie. The Place du Souvenir-Français is a predestined name for communities from elsewhere—predestined because the memories of the history of France unite these groups.

That Sunday, a pro-Palestinian rally turned violent. "Death to the Jews!" the marchers chanted. That day, I witnessed a kind of pogrom. The "pogrom," from the Russian *gromit*, meaning "to destroy," "to plunder," a word that appeared under the reign of the czars, had ravaged my native Poland and now had turned up here in France! Who would have believed it?

I feel like shouting, "Wake up!" For those people who aren't familiar with the Texts, I want to quote the Prophet

Muhammad: "He who loots or usurps, or encourages plundering, is not considered as one of us."[23]

Now, in Sarcelles, nothing is the same anymore. People speak to each other, but with distrust. Eyes meet, but they are filled with hostility.

A warning: Some people say Muslims are the bearers of a new anti-Semitism. Those who follow social media closely have reason to believe this is true. But what is "new" about this anti-Judaism being spit in our faces by our computer and smartphone screens?

Muslims do not have anti-Judaism theorists like Drumont, Maurras, or Bloy, no arguments elaborated by someone like Apion. Nor do they have theologians trying to differentiate themselves from the Judaism at their roots.

To attack the Jews, they have been forced to borrow the anti-Semitic discourse available to them, the one Europe has been drawing up for centuries. The one that is the most despicable and idiotic of all.

*

Freud believed the rejection of Jews originated from the other monotheistic religions, primarily Christians. For

---

23 English translation: Marcel Boisard, *Humanism in Islam*, trans. American Trust Publications (Plainfield, IN: American Trust Publications, 1988).

them it was a way to gain independence from the authority of the "father" by killing him (Oedipus complex).

The first Christians, as we know, were Jews. "I am not come to destroy but to fulfil," Jesus tells the temple guards, who he thinks are bad Jews for disrespecting both the rules of the Torah and the prophets' calls for justice. [24] With his apostles, Jesus speaks in Hebrew or Aramaic. In his small synagogue in Capernaum, on the northwest shore of the Sea of Galilee, he reads the psalms of David in Hebrew. Change comes with the arrival of the rabbi Saul of Tarsus, Saint Paul, who decides to appeal to the polytheistic Greeks and Romans because he knows the Jews will not follow Jesus. The timing is perfect: The Empire is experiencing an ideological crisis and Judaism is becoming attractive. But it is too complex. Saint Paul offers a simplified version of it—Christianity—using the idea from Leviticus of "love your neighbor as yourself" as its foundation, even though this precept will not always be respected by its adherents in later years. And it works.

David Ben-Gurion, the man who proclaimed the rebirth of Israel in 1948, liked to say that Jesus was the most brilliant figure in Jewish history. Which, incidentally, is how Saint Paul presents him to the pagans. But in order for him

---

24 Matthew 5:17 (KJV).

to be accepted by the majority, he would have to denounce the religion of the Jews, the very religion that had given him life. The process of disparaging the father that Freud talks about begins with him and will last for centuries.

Curiously, for Muhammad, founder of the third monotheistic religion six centuries later, the problem doesn't present itself in the same way. His situation is more like that of Luther, the reformer of Christianity in the sixteenth century. Faced with Christ the rebel son, who is now firmly planted in the landscape of faith, it is not enough to denounce the father; instead, he must be reclaimed. This is the reason the Prophet offers the Jews an alliance and that beautiful text by Safiya, the Constitution of Medina, written after the hijra in 622. Luther reminds readers of these origins in a short treatise entitled *That Jesus Christ Was Born a Jew* (1523).

But when someone believes, sincerely believes, why would he abandon his faith to embrace another? The Jews cling to their Texts. Worse still, the criticism from followers of the two other monotheisms only strengthens their faith. "Blind," the Catholics call them, representing them in their cathedrals as Synagoga ("Synagogue"), a sculpture of a woman wearing a blindfold and holding a broken scepter. This is true in Strasbourg, Bamberg, Worms, and Fribourg im Breisgau, towns located on both sides of the border between France and Germany. Then come the book-burnings and persecutions.

The people who scientifically planned for their physical elimination did not, we must concede, act in the name of their religious beliefs. Some were even borderline agnostic. Did they not say, as Nietzsche did, that "God is dead"?

So why, during the Second World War, did men who were not Nazis let them do it? Because, over the course of long centuries, our subconscious has been prepared, plowed, to accept the unacceptable. It seems to me that Goethe was right to say that "the Jew is the thermometer of the degree of humanity's humanity." The Nazis broke the thermometer, prompting Bernanos to declare in 1944: "Anti-Semite: this word increasingly fills me with horror. Hitler dishonored it once and for all."[25] He was mistaken. Seventy-five years later, individuals and groups of people are proudly using the same label. The list of reasons to hate Jews has simply been enriched with a few additional arguments—among them, Israel. For some, the problem is its politics; for others, its very existence. Not to mention all the people who support this state: the Zionists.

---

25 English translation: Maurice Samuels, *The Right to Difference: French Universalism and the Jews* (Chicago: University of Chicago Press, 2016).

5

A NEW TARGET: ISRAEL AND ZIONISM

"Zionism," like anti-Semitism, is a recent word. It is linked to the publication of *The Jewish State* in 1896 by Theodor Herzl, a Viennese correspondent who came to Paris to cover the Dreyfus trial, a case that would motivate Herzl's commitment to the cause. In an era when anti-colonial movements were being born—like the Indian National Congress, joined by Mahatma Gandhi in 1915, and the Wafd Party in Egypt, headed by Saad Zaghloul from 1919 onward—Herzl's essay legitimized the Jewish nationalist claim to Palestine, which was occupied first by the Ottomans and later by the British.

"Zionist Jews" are those in the Diaspora who support the Yishuv, the Jewish community in Palestine fighting for independence, despite the fact that, like any people or group demanding autonomy, it uses political and media pressure and terrorism alike to achieve its ends. In 1909, the Yishuv created the first Jewish militia, the Hashomer ("the watchman," responsible for defending new Jewish settlements in Palestine), followed by several paramilitary organizations: the Haganah (1920), the Palmach (1941), a labor movement, and the Irgun (1931) and the Stern (1940), two revisionist armed forces branches. We have the Irgun to thank for the dynamiting of the King David Hotel in Jerusalem on July 22, 1946, that left behind so many victims.

The Arab Palestinians would follow suit years later by creating groups such as the Fatah (or Palestine National Liberation Movement, which claims to be socialist) in 1959, the Popular Front for the Liberation of Palestine (1967, grounded in Marxist ideology), and the Democratic Front for the Liberation of Palestine (1969, grounded in Maoism).

The partition of Palestine was adopted by the UN in 1947, the same time that India became independent. The Jews declared the establishment of their state in 1948. The histories of India and the State of Israel intersect, as correspondence between Ben-Gurion and Gandhi can attest. To Gandhi's great despair, in an attempt to preserve its power before disappearing, the British Empire obtained the partition of colonial India, just like what had been done in Palestine. On one side was Muslim Pakistan, on the other Hindu India.

The birth of Israel poses a problem for anti-Semites, most of whom wanted to see Jews leave Europe for Palestine. So they make a distinction between the Israelis and the Jews from their own countries, who are English, French, Belgian, etc.: Israelis are "the others." These "others" who, after the Holocaust, they cannot reasonably attack or persecute. Unless they can call the Holocaust into question! Prove that it never existed or that it wasn't what the survivors say it was. These new anti-Semites are "negationists." In their eyes, the Jews in the Diaspora are using their suffering to insert themselves into various strata of Western society: the media, the economy, politics.

The birth of any nation, like that of any person, is a painful process, often provoking chain reactions and conflicts, some of which endure. The dispute between India and Pakistan concerning the Kashmir is one example. Another is the conflict between the Israelis and the Palestinians, the latter of whom are still without their own state.

*

One could say that after more than seventy years of existence, Israel has become a *normal* country.

I remember an argument I had about this with David
Ben-Gurion.

It was in 1967 or 1968. The State's old founding father
had been living on a remote kibbutz in the heart of the
Negev desert, Sde Boker, since 1953. After our dinner
together, Ben Gurio accompanied me by car to Tel Aviv.
His car was comfortable but not air-conditioned, so the
windows had been rolled down to let in a breeze. At a red
light, not far from the former opera house where he had
celebrated the proclamation of the State of Israel on May
14, 1948, a young woman approached the car, leaned over
to me, and said in Yiddish, "*Dou kimst?*" ("You coming?")

A Jewish prostitute! And one who spoke my mother's
language! I was shaken. Seeing me upset, Ben-Gurion
started laughing.

"You see, we've finally become a normal people!" he
crowed, slapping his thigh. "I bet we even have our own
thieves!"

His remark exasperated me even more than the young
woman's proposition. I flew into a rage and the driver
almost rammed into a bus.

"But David, I don't want to be normal!"

*

I didn't know at the time that I was reinventing the age-old debate between the Jews of Israel and those of the Diaspora, an opposition that is also found in the two Talmuds ("study" in Hebrew): the Jerusalem Talmud and the Babylonian Talmud.

The former is marked by the definitive loss of independence in 130 CE and the failure of the final Jewish revolt against Rome (the Bar Kokhba Rebellion). Emperor Hadrian did not forgive this rebellious people for standing up to him. To radically punish the Jews, he decided to wipe them off the map, even down to their names: Jerusalem became Aelia Capitolina and Judea was rebaptized as Palestine (Palaestina in Latin).

In the face of this fury, the sages of Israel feared the wealth of words, reflections, and rules they guarded would also be erased. They decided to transcribe them immediately into a book. After a lengthy gestation, the text was completed in around 426 CE. But the sense of urgency that swept through the sages in Jerusalem during Hadrian's time was felt far beyond Judea. It touched the entire Jewish Diaspora. The academies in Babylon, where the community born out of the first exile in 598 BCE had developed and flourished in the meantime, also started working.

A century after the Jerusalem Talmud, a second text known as the Babylonian Talmud emerged. Written in exile, it was naturally more focused on relations with the surrounding peoples than the Jerusalem Talmud. It is there-fore more universal. It presents itself less as a code of laws for practical daily decisions and more as an encyclopedic account of often contradictory discussions on a broad range of themes: astronomy, anatomy, psychology, medicine. This is why, during the time of Rabelais, it was an integral part of medical teaching at the University of Montpellier, and why the author of *Gargantua and Pantagruel* knew Hebrew so well.

Yes, I admit it—Ben-Gurion was right. Israel has indeed become a "normal" state. But, as Nietzsche writes in *Thus Spoke Zarathustra*, "State is the name of the coldest of all cold monsters."[26] It can equip itself with institutions that protect it from drifting off course, but not from Evil. This is why the sages of biblical times invented the prophets: to challenge the kings and priests. In fact, by referencing these prophets in their critique of injustices being committed

---

26 English translation: Friedrich Nietzsche, *Thus Spoke Zarathustra: A Book for All and None*, trans. Adrian Del Caro (Cambridge: Cambridge University Press, 2006).

in their countries, and by claiming to be the guardians of the Ten Commandments, the Jews in the Diaspora gave anti-Zionists arguments to use against Israel, a state that, like all states, cannot guarantee their protection.

Anti-Semitism and anti-Zionism. The Jewish people consider them one and the same, and with reason. For as Jean-Paul Sartre said, whoever detests Jews is inevitably a criminal, since what he wishes and plans for is their death.

For anti-Semites, the death of Jews. For anti-Zionists, the death of Israel.

6

WHAT IF IT ALL STARTED WITH THE TEN COMMANDMENTS?

What if these biblical commands, and the concept of being their bearers, are at the very root of the rejection of Jews?

Let's review the history. Contrary to Freud's belief that anti-Semitism began with Christianity, when we reread the Texts, we discover that hostility toward Jews appeared well before the birth of Christianity—and, consequently, that of Islam.

Does it date back to Abraham and the birth of monotheism, as some historians claim? Not at all. Back when every tribe had its own god, or gods, the One God of Abraham was considered by his contemporaries to be just one more. Invisible, yes, but nothing to call into question their own beliefs. Thus the king of Salem, Melchizedek, welcomed Abraham and his tribe like brothers, as did Abimelech, king of the Philistine city Gerar, with whom he signed a pact of friendship near Be'er Sheva. And from the Hittite Ephron, Abraham bought the parcel of land near the Cave of Machpelah in Hebron, where he buried his wife Sarah and where he himself would be laid to rest: the Tomb of the Patriarchs.

The first anti-Jewish texts appeared with Moses. With the slaves' first revolt and their departure from Egypt, emptying its cities and countryside of a third of their population. The target of this rejection was in fact the Ten Commandments (or Decalogue). This text, which goes against human customs and traditions of the time, is probably the most dissident text ever written to date. So much so that even the Jewish tradition relates how difficult it was for the people of Israel to accept these Commandments.

*

The Texts say that when God devises the Ten Commandments, he wonders who he will give them to. He remembers the sons of Esau and speaks to them. They immediately ask him: "What do these Commandments require?"

"You shall not murder," the Eternal says.

"No, thank you," the sons of Esau reply. "That would mean renouncing the blessing of our Father, who when he left us said, 'You will live by the sword.'"

The Eternal then turned to the sons of Ammon and Moab.

"What do your Commandments require?" they ask him.

"Six days you shall do your work, but on the seventh day you shall cease from labor."

"How will we survive when seven days of labor is already not enough to feed us?"

So the Eternal asks the other nations, but all of them find his Commandments too restrictive. They suggest that he offer his laws to the people of Israel, who are wandering in the desert and have nothing to lose. The Eternal thinks this is a good idea and calls upon Moses: "Go and ask the Hebrews if they will accept the Ten Commandments."

Moses dedicates himself to the task and goes to speak to the women first. Indeed, the Talmud explains, if Eve had not desired the fruit from the tree of knowledge, Adam would have never disobeyed his own leader. He would have remained ignorant. And all of humanity with him. No curiosity, no school, no university, no research. . . . Men owe everything to this original woman's thirst for wisdom.

Aware that the women are the first link in the transmission of knowledge, Moses makes sure he has their support. He then gathers the Jewish people together.

"Will you accept the Ten Commandments?" he asks.

"We will," the Hebrews answer. "And whatever He commands, we will do it!"

Moses is wary of such rapid commitment.

"Who will be the guardians of your promise before God?"

"Our ancestors."

"Your ancestors are dead; how can they be your guardians?"

"Our prophets, then."

"Your prophets haven't been born yet," Moses replies. "How can they be your guardians?"

Then the women intervene.

"Our children will be our guardians," they suggest. "The Eternal will teach you the Torah and you will teach it to the fathers. Then the fathers will transmit it to the children, and the children to their children."

Moses turns to the children. "Do you agree to be your parents' guardians?"

"We will do it," they reply.

And this, the story concludes, is how the Jews received the Torah.

*

I imagine that Moses faced two problems while carving the Ten Commandments in stone: not only did he have to invent a non-image expression corresponding to the abstract idea of a unique God, he also had to think about how to unify the disparate mob awaiting his return at the foot of Mount Sinai.

Moses was also obligated to consider the various beliefs at work in the hearts of these men and women, their recent history, their experience, and their capacity for understanding and anticipation. The finished text is even more admirable when we keep this unusual context in mind.

The Ten Commandments begin with a basic premise: the Lord is God, the Lord is One, and He is the sole Creator of the Earth, the heavens, and mankind.

This God, as we have seen, immediately places humanity on the path of history: "I am the LORD, the God of your fathers." And He continues: "I the LORD am your God who brought you out of the land of Egypt, the house of bondage."[27]

---

27 Exodus 20:2.

These few lines represent the most extraordinary shortcut in human thought. In two paragraphs, men discover that they are inscribed in time, part of a larger picture. And not in some arbitrary way: They are free! God took them out of "the house of bondage." In so doing, He also shows that time belongs to humanity as a potential tool of liberation.

Freedom, however, permits everything: both Good and Evil. As well as submission, to man just as much as to the forces of nature, which is simply another form of slavery.

I believe it was in thinking about all this that Moses carved the third and fourth Commandments: "You shall have no other gods besides Me"[28] and "You shall not make for yourself a sculptured image, or any likeness of what is in the heavens above, or on the earth below, or in the waters under the earth [...]. You shall not bow down to them or serve them."[29]

Which idols is Moses alluding to? Those representing the forces of nature, of course: wild animals, yes, but also their bestial human versions, those tyrants and dictators who are constantly born and reborn—the pharaohs, the future Caligulas, and the immense cohort that culminates in Hitler, Stalin, Pol Pot, and Ceauşescu.

---

28 Exodus 20:3.

29 Exodus 20:4 and 5.

Ultimately, there is no freedom without the meaning of freedom—the Law, in other words. And there is no law in the "house of bondage." Idols loom constantly before us and we must resist them at all times.

Here Moses sensed another danger: submission to the Lord Himself, to Him who created us and liberated us from slavery. This is why he added: "You shall not swear falsely by the name of the LORD your God."[30] Which, nonetheless, we all do, without exception. Who among us has never said, "Make this happen!" or "God willing," whether in French, Hebrew, or Arabic? And often for trivial reasons.

From this point on, Moses could speak to men as responsible beings. This is why the following Commandment introduced for the first time, to my knowledge, a social rule that would prove to be essential: "Six days you shall labor and do all your work, but the seventh day is a sabbath of the LORD your God [Shabbat]; you shall not do any work—you, your son or your daughter, your male or female slave, your ox or your ass, or any of your cattle, or the stranger in your settlements."[31] "Remember that you were a slave in the land of Egypt."[32]

---

30 Exodus 20:7.

31 Deuteronomy 5:13 and 14.

32 Deuteronomy 5:15.

Thousands of years before the first union demands, a man invented the six-day work week with a day of rest for everyone, including the woman—who in this way became man's equal—including the slave, and including the foreigner! We can imagine what such a law must have represented at the time of Moses, when at the beginning of the last century it still seemed too revolutionary here in France.

Further, some Jewish thinkers like the late German psychologist Erich Fromm believe that the spiritual and moral survival of Jews over the course of these two thousand years of persecution and humiliation would hardly have been possible without this day of the week on which the poorest and most underprivileged finds himself transformed into a dignified and proud being, the beggar into a king.

It would take too long to analyze the other Commandments here. Some of them we know well—"You shall not murder," "Honor your mother and father"—and they are now part of almost all the constitutions of the world.

*

During his forty years of wandering in the desert, Moses tried repeatedly to enact not only the Ten Commandments but an entire set of laws dedicated to daily practices. And so, before dying, he bequeathed to us an extraordinary moral code: "You shall not wrong a stranger or oppress him, for you were strangers in the land of Egypt. You shall not ill-treat any widow or orphan."[33]

"You shall not abuse a needy and destitute laborer, whether a fellow countryman or a stranger in one of the communities of your land. You must pay him his wages on the same day, before the sun sets, for he is needy and urgently depends on it."[34]

Remember—these words were written around thirty-five hundred years ago!

Moses continued: "When you reap the harvest in your field and overlook a sheaf in the field, do not turn back to get it; it shall go to the stranger, the fatherless, and the widow."[35]

"You shall [not] side with the mighty to do wrong; [and] you shall not give perverse testimony in a dispute so as to pervert it in favor of the mighty."[36]

---

33 Exodus 22:20 and 21.

34 Deuteronomy 24:14 and 15.

35 Deuteronomy 24:19.

36 Exodus 23:2.

7

"THE JEWISH PEOPLE"
—A PROVOCATION?

I suspect that Moses, like all great legislators, also had in mind the organization of a Jewish society in his land. His final words attest to his legitimate sadness at having been unable to achieve it. I would characterize the society he hoped for as a "biblical democracy," as opposed to "Athenian democracy."

In Athens, equality only pertained to member citizens of the same caste who came together on the agora to resolve their differences. The others—women, multiracial people, slaves, and foreigners—who represented the majority of the population were excluded from the city. Plato even wanted to keep out the poets, whom he considered liars.

"Biblical democracy," on the other hand, is for everyone. In Jewish thought, all people are equal, since all were created in the image of the Lord, regardless of physical appearance. This biblical democracy is built on three pillars: politics, religion, and civil society. Politics was governed by kings. Religion was managed by priests chosen from the tribe of Levi, which is why they were called Levites. Their first chief was Aaron, brother of Moses. Thus, for the first time in history, we see a distinction made between religion and the state. When Jesus utters the now famous words, "Render therefore unto Caesar the things which are Caesar's; and unto God the things that are God's," he is still Jewish.

To whom is Moses offering—or perhaps it is better to say, on whom is he imposing—these Commandments? A crowd of men and women who have found themselves together by chance. Were they following a desire for freedom? Or, as Hegel believed, a wish to take their turn as masters? Were they perhaps simply united by the rejection of slavery? Among them, of course, are Hebrews, children of Abraham, Isaac, and Jacob. But there are also children of the famous Joseph, Jacob's eleventh son, whose brothers sold him as a slave to a caravan of Ishmaelite merchants who brought him to Egypt. There, under the reign of the Hyksos (Semites like the Hebrews), who occupied the country between 1674 and 1548 BCE, Joseph is appointed viceroy and becomes Pharaoh's confidant, thanks to his prophetic visions. But the majority of the people who form this colorful crowd are other slaves belonging to tribes conquered by Egypt, including members of the tribe of Jethro—father of Zipporah, the wife of Moses—who were African and black, or *cushi*, the Bible says.

According to the Text (Numbers 2:32), the first census in history records 603,550 men between the ages of twenty and forty, capable of defending themselves against the hostile tribes waiting to ambush them on the road leading to the Promised Land. If to these 603,550 men we add women, the elderly, and children, I believe we could reasonably arrive at three million souls. An immense crowd in the desert, just as Cecil B. DeMille imagined in his 1956 Hollywood film *The Ten Commandments*.

*

Not long ago, after my conference at the Festival du Livre in Nice, a man stuck out his hand to me.

"Are you prepared to shake my hand?" he asked me.

"Who are you?"

"Shlomo Sand, Israeli historian."

"I shake everyone's hand. We don't have to agree with each other."

This is a man who defends the idea that the Jews do not constitute a people—and therefore, that they do not deserve a state. Yet, in addition to the fact that many states today are founded on religion alone, such as Pakistan and Saudi Arabia, the Jews are very much a people that Moses formed out of this diverse throng 3,500 years ago by giving them the gift of the Law. Don't dictionaries define "a people" as "a body of persons that typically have common language, institutions, and beliefs, and that often constitute a politically organized group"?[37] With this gesture, Moses handed the Jews not only a framework and a history, but also—and this is essential in this particular case—the notion of freedom. This "difficult freedom" (Essays on Judaism by the philoshopher Emmanuel Levinas, 1906-1995) men dread and against which, the Bible tells us, these people in formation at the foot of Mount Sinai revolt.

A visionary quoted in forty-four surahs in the Qur'an, Moses understood that freedom is a long learning process. So he allowed all the former slaves to perish in the desert, counting on the new generation, born free, to build a nation.

---

37 *Merriam-Webster's Dictionary.*

The Qur'an quotes Moses as saying: "O my people, enter the Holy Land which Allah has assigned to you and do not turn back and become losers."[38] "And We said after Pharaoh to the Children of Israel, 'Dwell in the land, and when there comes the promise of the Hereafter, We will bring you forth in [one] gathering.'"[39]

*

"Freedom at last!" I exclaimed the first time I met Andreï Dmitrievich Sakharov. It was 1988. I had traveled to Moscow at his invitation. He wanted to thank me personally for the campaign I had conducted with Mistislav Rostropovich to lend support after his exile to Gorky by the KGB.

"Freedom," he replied, "is like an orange. A person who has never seen an orange will never think of asking for one. We must first make young Russian people aware of the existence of this exotic fruit, explain its qualities. Only then, perhaps, out of curiosity or out of yearning, will our youth go out into the streets to ask for oranges."

"It's an education problem, then," I responded.

---

38 Qur'an 5:21.
39 Qur'an 17:104.

"That's true. But our schools and universities are part of the old regime. None of them would allow the orange to be endorsed. We need a Western university, the first in the Soviet Union . . ."

After thinking a moment, he said, "Why not a French one?"

Then he laughed, adding, "Now you know what you have to do, Marek Halter."

"Me? My dear Andreï Sakharov, I only went to school for six months. I don't know what a university is!"

Sakharov swept away my argument with his hand. "Yes, but you know what an orange is!"

In Moses's time, the orange, which would not reach the Mediterranean region until the Middle Ages, did not exist. Neither did freedom. But the peerless lawmaker must nevertheless arouse a desire for it. Well, what desire could impel these former slaves? Certainly not freedom. They weren't familiar with it. Not only were the Ten Commandments difficult for them to follow, they also provoked hostility from all the neighboring peoples.

Rebellion, therefore, was to be expected. "What have you done to us, taking us out of Egypt?" they asked Moses. "Let us be, and we will serve the Egyptians, for it is better for us to serve the Egyptians than to die in the wilderness."[40]

---

40 Exodus 14:11 and 12.

Let's remember God's anger at the foolishness of the mob worshipping the golden calf. "I see that this is a stiff-necked people," the Eternal groaned to Moses, who broke the Tablets of the Law.[41] But then he pulled himself together. Perhaps he understood that he must be the first— even in the worst circumstances—to practice the humanity he professed to uphold, according to which no trial is acceptable if it does not produce profound meaning in the hearts of men.

So Moses once again climbed Mount Sinai and for forty days and forty nights he followed God's dictates and carved the second version of the Commandments.

I have often wondered why it had been necessary for Moses to carve the same Laws a second time. After all, he could have very easily gotten angry without breaking the stone Tablets. Moreover, the two versions appear at first glance to be nearly identical.

However, there is one important difference. It concerns the observance of the Sabbath: "Six days you shall work, but on the seventh day you shall cease from labor; you shall cease from labor even at plowing time and harvest time."[42] In the first version, to institute the "day of rest," Moses

---

41 Exodus 32:9.

42 Exodus 34:21.

67

referenced the rest God took after creating the world in six days.[43] In the second, as recorded in Deuteronomy, he used the memory of slavery in Egypt.[44]

We can see in this shift an impulse to make man alone responsible for the Commandments that concern him. Just when the Hebrews in the bottom of the valley were ready to renounce their freedom and return under the yoke of Egypt, their liberation from Pharaoh's grasp becomes the very object of remembrance and meditation for the Sabbath day.

In a way, the first version of the Ten Commandments is God's, and the second becomes humanity's. Thus the Text would suggest that it is men, drawing upon their experience, who decide their own rules, which implies that they do not submit to them out of devotion or adoration. Therefore, these rules can never serve idolatry. The result is a statement that is fundamental to the spirit of Judaism: the Law was given out of love for man, and not out of love and submission to a God, even if he is the Eternal.

---

43 Exodus 20:11.

44 Deuteronomy 5:15.

8

MOSES: THE ONE
WHO BRINGS SCANDAL

The Sabbath is, without a doubt, the institution that most surprises the pagans. In his poem "The Itinerary, or Journal of a Voyage from Rome to Gaul," for instance, Rutilius Numatianus speaks of

> The foul race [...]
> Root of fond folly, who their Sabbaths hold,
> With hearts, as is their superstition, cold;
> Who each seventh day in sloth ignobly lie,
> Soft image of a wearied deity [...]

With wide contagion creeps the outrooted pest,
The conquerors by the conquered tribe opprest.[45]

Several Greek authors also point out that if Jerusalem was taken four times, it was because the Jews refused to defend themselves on the Sabbath. Apion, an Alexandrian grammarian in the first century—against whom Jewish historian Flavius Josephus wrote an entire book—claimed that the word "Shabbat," etymologically, comes from the Egyptian *sabbatosis*, meaning "groin pain." According to him, the Hebrews, led by Moses out of Egypt, would have been afflicted with groin tumors after six days of walking and were forced, as a result, to rest on the seventh day.

This theory echoes those of several Egyptian writers regarding Jews' "impurity." In the third century BCE, Egyptian priest Manetho made this the basis for one of his own theories. He claimed that the Hebrews, exiled by Pharaoh, were in fact lepers, blind, crippled, and covered in sores, a hypothesis repeated by Posidonius of Apamea and Lysimachus of Alexandria. Even Plutarch endorsed the idea as a way to explain the Jews' abstention from pork, which he said was for hygienic reasons since pigs are leprous and

---

45 English translation: Charles Abraham Elton, *Specimens of the Greek and Roman Classic Poets, in Chronological Series from Homer to Tryphiodorus, Volume III* (Philadelphia: F. Bell, 1854).

mangy: ". . . the Jews apparently abominate pork because barbarians especially abhor skin diseases like lepra and white scale, and believe that human beings are ravaged by such maladies through contagion."[46]

It is not astonishing that the Greek Strabo, a contemporary of Jesus, considered the Jews a pernicious nation, especially since they are, in fact, universally widespread. "It is not easy to find any place in the habitable world which has not received this nation and in which it has not made its power felt."[47] Indeed, after the destruction of the First Temple by the Babylonians in 587 BCE, the Jews were scattered across the world, united primarily by their attachment to the Ten Commandments and respect for the Sabbath.

Historians believe that this Diaspora—a Greek word—was quite sizable: five to six million Jews, including one and a half million in Palestine, out of the Roman Empire's total population of sixty million people.

This dispersal was what helped the Jewish people survive, since no one, including Hitler, could be everywhere at the same time. On the other hand, this dissemination fueled the belief in a Jewish conspiracy to take over the world via

---

46 English translation: Jack N. Lightstone and Herbert W. Basser, *The Commerce of the Sacred: Mediation of the Divine Among Jews in the Greco-Roman World* (New York: Columbia University Press, 2006).

47 English translation: Moyer V. Hubbard, *Christianity in the Greco-Roman World: A Narrative Introduction* (Grand Rapids, MI: Baker Academic, 2010).

control of the banking system and by financing revolutions and coups d'état. Hence the success, during the Occupation in France, of the collaborationist and anti-Semitic newspaper *Je suis partout* ("I am everywhere")—a precursor to our fake news sites—which was directed by a group of Charles Maurras supporters that included Robert Brasillach. It was this weekly publication that launched, among other things, the idea of the "cosmopolitan" Jew, who is detached from any sense of patriotism toward the country in which he lives.

This is false, of course. One need only cite the example of Marc Bloch, the historian who revolutionized the teaching of history with the Annales School he and Lucien Lefebvre created. A member of the Resistance, arrested by the Gestapo and sentenced to death, when standing in front of the firing squad he let out a cry that encapsulated the condition of Jews in a country where they had lived for centuries: "*Vive la France! Vive les Prophètes d'Israël!*"

Romain Gary once said he felt like a foreigner in France and like a Frenchman in other countries. I, for one, feel at home everywhere, and everywhere French (perhaps because I dream in French). I also feel Jewish, precisely because of the Ten Commandments. And the Sabbath. These Commandments and this Sabbath that so terrify totalitarian and authoritarian systems. For proof of this, read the words of Seneca as cited by Léon Poliakov in *The History of Anti-Semitism*: "The practices of this villainous nation have so greatly prevailed that they are accepted throughout the universe; the vanquished have given laws unto the victors."[48]

He may not be wrong. These Laws, these Ten Commandments that I have spent so much time discussing, and this Sabbath represent the most subversive and revolutionary idea in history. Michelet says of the Jews in *History of the French Revolution* (volume III, chapter 2): "These ancestors of Christianity, so harshly treated by their own sons, were also, in one sense, the ancestors of the French Revolution; the latter, as a reaction of Right, would necessarily bow down before that austere law, wherein Moses foresaw the future triumph of Right."[49] These Laws are difficult to obey for the people who claim to be their guardians, and difficult to accept for the states those people live in.

Incidentally, when the revolutionaries of 1789 were searching for a format for their Declaration of the Rights of Man—something all the citizens of the new Republic would be able to understand—they naturally chose, as anticlerical as they were, the Tablets of the Law of Moses.

---

48 English translation: Léon Poliakov, *The History of Anti-Semitism, Volume I: From the Time of Christ to the Court Jews*, trans. Richard Howard (Philadelphia: University of Pennsylvania Press, 2003).

49 English translation: Jules Michelet, *History of the French Revolution*, trans. Charles Cocks (Chicago: University of Chicago Press, 1967).

When my parents and I arrived in Paris in 1950, not knowing the language, I used to admire the image of these "Tablets of the Law" that, at the time, adorned police stations around the city. One day I even naively asked my uncle David, who had brought us to France, whether it meant that the French police captains were Jewish. The "Tablets of the Law" have since deserted the police stations. Too dangerous?

Every society throughout history has encountered subversive ideas and the people who are their bearers. This often leads to uprisings, revolts, and revolutions. Well, what was subversive yesterday becomes conservative the day after, and as Hegel posits, the conservative system born from yesterday's subversion in turn arouses protests of its own.

The Jews, by labeling themselves as such—albeit often involuntarily—represent not a protest against circumstance, but a *permanent* protest. They are therefore dangerous. "Like the plague," Freud writes.

*

As I quote the Viennese psychoanalyst, I experience a kind of illumination. I have just understood why, while Hitler took power in Germany and began his project of cleansing Europe of its Jewish presence, Freud, of Jewish origin himself, put forth his final completed book, *Moses and Monotheism.*[50] Moses, according to him, would not have been a Jew, but an Egyptian who had close ties to Pharaoh Ikhnaton and would have been assassinated by the Jews: ". . . my hypothesis that Moses was not a Jew, but an Egyptian, creates a new enigma. What he did—easily understandable if he were a Jew—becomes unintelligible in an Egyptian. But if we place Moses in Ikhnaton's period and associate him with that Pharaoh, then the enigma is resolved and a possible motive presents itself, answering all our questions. Let us assume that Moses was a noble and distinguished man, perhaps indeed a member of the royal house, as the myth has it. He must have been conscious of his great abilities, ambitious, and energetic; perhaps he saw himself in a dim future as the leader of his people, the governor of the Empire. In close contact with Pharaoh, he was a convinced adherent of the new religion, whose basic principles he fully understood and had made his own." Really?

Moses is certainly fascinating, especially to anti-Semites. We pay so much attention to manifestations of modern anti-Judaism, which draw their hatred from post-Judaic religions and extreme ideologies on the hunt for scapegoats, that we have never taken a look back at the legislator of

---

50 English translation: Sigmund Freud, *Moses and Monotheism*, trans. Katherine Jones (New York: Vintage Books, 1967).

Judaism himself. The man who, by entrusting the Jews with upholding the dream of justice and freedom for all men, rendered them forever subversive and incapable of living under oppressive regimes—and becoming, consequently, their greatest victims.

There is no such thing as chance: At the very moment I am revisiting this manuscript, a friend brings me a book he found at a used bookstore: *Letters of Certain Jews to Monsieur Voltaire*. It is a fifth edition copy, printed in 1782—an edition that angered the author of the *Treatise on Tolerance*, in which he demonstrates so little tolerance toward Jews. Voltaire deems these letters "impudent, uncivil, adapted only to critics without taste." "Your trifling satire will be disregarded by genteel people of some learning," he adds.[51]

Reading this rather arrogant judgement prompted me to reread Voltaire's text, and it seems to me that, failing to honestly critique the Ten Commandments—whose meaning, I imagine, the Enlightenment philosopher could appreciate—he decided to attack their alleged "author," just as Freud did many years later and for other reasons. According to Voltaire, Moses could not have carved the Ten Commandments and therefore could not have written the

---

51 English translation: Antoine Guénée, *Letters of Certain Jews to Monsieur Voltaire*, trans. Philip Le Fanu (Philadelphia: H. Hooker; Cincinnati: G.G. Jones, 1848).

Pentateuch for, as the philosopher explained, to communicate, the Egyptians at the time used hieroglyphics!

Having written a book myself on Zipporah, Moses's black wife, I had had to dive into period documents that were already known about in Voltaire's time and that prove the use of the cuneiform alphabet, which was invented by the Chaldeans under the Sumerian Empire and adopted by the Jews during the time of Abraham. Poor Moses! So admired by Michelangelo, yet also the man Freud wanted to subtract from Jewish lineage in order to save the Jews from Nazi hatred.

Freud was highly intelligent and knew that his theory would rouse the hostility of all the historians and all the archaeologists of his time, not to mention the Jews, whom he was stripping of their identity. So why did he undertake such a questionable venture?

When Freud was very young, biographer Ernest Jones writes in *The Daily Life of Freud*, he was traumatized by an anti-Semitic attack. He was walking with his father in the streets of Vienna when they were insulted by a thug. The man grabbed his father's hat and threw it in the gutter. His father said nothing. He picked up his hat, dusted it off, and put it back on his head.

I imagine that Freud, as I did years later, must have wondered, "Why?" Why the Jews? Why anti-Semitism? And that he arrived at the same conclusion I did: because of Moses and his Ten Commandments, embodied and upheld by Jews around the world. Freud then set out to do something crazy, suicidal: He decided to save the Jews from themselves. By demonstrating to the anti-Semites not that they were mistaken, but that they had chosen the wrong targets.

A misguided approach. A bad book. Burned by the Nazis in the public squares along with other works believed to be "degenerate." Freud's diagnosis was correct, but the remedy was deadly.

9

ARE WE TRAPPED?

Perhaps. Trapped: The Jews who adopted Moses's pact, because this is what they have always been reproached for. Trapped: The non-Jews for whom the mere presence of these "close strangers" among them serves as a ceaseless reprimand.

Are we, as Sartre claims, only what we are "through the eyes of the other"?

The choice seems simple: Accept the Jews as they are and reexamine ourselves, or instead reject them and prove them right. To avoid this choice, we disregard their principles and throw it back in their faces. Is this why the Synagoga statue is blindfolded in French churches? To avoid meeting her gaze?

What should we do? Remove the blindfold? Restore the Jews' sight? This would mean agreeing to meet their gaze, even to change society. Beginning with a decision to admit to the breadth of its diversity.

And in the meantime? The Jew could certainly stop being Jewish. Deny his memory and his Commandments, change his religion (for those who are practicing). Change his name, too—why not? Until one day a new Hitler reminds his descendants of their origins. He could also leave the country of his birth for Israel and become "normal."

*

We are living in a strange time: the passage from one world to another. At least in terms of technology. And climate.

The Hebrew Bible contains three sections: the Pentateuch (history and the Law, or history of the Law), the Prophets (texts written by visionary men who warned leaders about the changing world), and the Writings.

Today, there are no more prophets. There are only leaders who enact laws and writers to comment on them. And without prophets, there are no more dreams. Only crises to be handled.

Curiously, the Jews are often, and unintentionally, among the few who do still carry a dream. Do they not defend the dream of a society that is more just, more sustainable, more united, in which they could survive as Jews? Our aimless world, devoid of collective desire, will soon lose patience with this people rooted in a Book that touts the idea of a new relationship between man and nature.

"The wolf shall dwell with the lamb," Isaiah says, "[and] the leopard lie down with the kid. And the lion, like the ox, shall eat straw."[52] "For waters shall burst forth in the desert, Streams in the wilderness. Torrid earth shall become a pool; Parched land, fountains of water."[53] And Hosea adds: "In that day, I will make a covenant for them with the beasts of the field, the birds of the air, and the creeping things of the ground; I will also banish bow, sword, and war from the land. Thus I will let them lie down in safety."[54]

But before humanity comes together, before it rediscovers the Texts, the increasingly rapid changes in our environment and the scarcity of perspectives will accentuate the pressure from extremes and feed people's fear of the future.

And so, I believe, the Jews of the dispersal will have to endure more and more demonstrations of hostility. Regardless of Israeli politics, and even if the peace I have always fought for comes to pass with the Palestinians. The

52 Isaiah 11:6 and 7.

53 Isaiah 35:6 and 7.

54 Hosea 2:20.

only thing left for them to do, as they have done at other times, will be to find a certain glory in this role of the sacrificial victim, one that is necessary—as we saw with the "scapegoat" figure—for the survival of any society that is afraid.

Pope John Paul II, for whom I had such great appreciation, stood before a crowd of young Catholics on the Place Saint-Pierre on October 22, 1978, and cried out, "Do not be afraid!" He was right. For only a society without fear, a society that has no need for a "lightning rod" (Jules Michelet, 1798–1874), would accept the Jew, as he is, as one of its own, and consider him a brother.

ACKNOWLEDGMENTS

Thank you to Sophie Jaulmes for assisting me throughout the writing of this text and for verifying the dates and quotations that appear within it.

ACKNOWLEDGEMENTS

BY THE SAME AUTHOR

- *Le Fou et les Rois*, Albin Michel, 1976
  Prix Aujourd'hui 1976
  Published in English: *The Jester and the Kings: A Political Autobiography*, trans. Lowell Bair (Arcade Publishing, 1989)

- *La Mémoire d'Abraham*, Robert Laffont, 1983
  Prix du Livre Inter 1984
  Published in English: *The Book of Abraham*, trans. Lowell Bair (Dell Publishing Co., 1987)

- *Les Fils d'Abraham*, Robert Laffont, 1989
  Published in English: *The Children of Abraham*, trans. Lowell Bair (Arcade Publishing, 1990)

- *Un homme, un cri*, Robert Laffont, 1991

- *Les Fous de la paix* (with Éric Laurent), Plon/Robert Laffont, 1994

- *La Force du Bien*, Robert Laffont, 1995
  Grand Prix du livre de Toulon pour l'ensemble de l'œuvre (1995)
  Published in English: *Stories of Deliverance: Speaking with Men and Women Who Rescued Jews from the Holocaust*, trans. Michael Bernard (Carus Publishing Company, 1998)

- *Les Mystères de Jérusalem*, Robert Laffont, 1999
  Prix Océanes 2000

- *Le Judaïsme raconté à mes filleuls*, Robert Laffont, 1999

- *Le Vent des Khazars*, Robert Laffont, 2001
  Published in English: *The Wind of the Khazars*, trans. Michael Bernard (Toby Press, 2003)

- *Sarah–La Bible au féminin*, Robert Laffont, 2003
  Published in English: *Sarah: A Novel–Book One of the Canaan Trilogy*, trans. Howard Curtis (Crown Publishers, 2004)

- *Tsippora–La Bible au féminin*, Robert Laffont, 2003
  Published in English: *Zipporah, Wife of Moses–Book Two of the Canaan Trilogy*, trans. Howard Curtis (Crown Publishers, 2005)

- *Lilah–La Bible au féminin*, Robert Laffont, 2004
  Published in English: *Lilah: A Forbidden Love, A People's Destiny–Book Three of the Canaan Trilogy*, trans. Howard Curtis (Crown Publishers, 2006)

- *Marie*, Robert Laffont, 2006
  Published in English: *Mary of Nazareth*, trans. Howard Curtis (Crown Publishers, 2008)

- *Je me suis réveillé en colère*, Robert Laffont, 2007

- *La Reine de Saba*, Robert Laffont, 2008
  Prix Femmes de paix 2009

- *Le Kabbaliste de Prague*, Robert Laffont, 2010

- *L'Inconnue de Birobidjan*, Robert Laffont, 2012

- *Faites-le!*, Kero, 2013

- *Khadija–Les Femmes de l'islam*, Robert Laffont, 2014

- *Réconciliez-vous!*, Robert Laffont, 2015
  Prix pour la Culture méditerranéenne 2015

- *Fatima–Les Femmes de l'islam*, Robert Laffont, 2015

- *Aïcha–Les Femmes de l'islam*, Robert Laffont, 2015

- *Ève*, Robert Laffont, 2016

- *Où allons-nous, mes amis?*, Robert Laffont, 2017

- *Je rêvais de changer le monde–Mémoires*, Robert Laffont, 2019
  Prix du Livre de l'année 2019 Gonzague Saint Bris